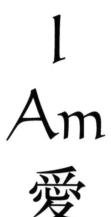

I Am 愛

{I Am Love}

José L. Gomez Jr.

BALBOA.
PRESS.

A DIVISION OF HAY HOUSE

Balboa Press books may be ordered through booksellers or by contacting:

Balboa Press
A Division of Hay House
1663 Liberty Drive
Bloomington, IN 47403
www.balboapress.com
1-(877) 407-4847

Because of the dynamic nature of the Internet, any web addresses or
links contained in this book may have changed since publication and
may no longer be valid. The views expressed in this work are solely those
of the author and do not necessarily reflect the views of the publisher,
and the publisher hereby disclaims any responsibility for them.

The author of this book does not dispense medical advice or prescribe the use
of any technique as a form of treatment for physical, emotional, or medical
problems without the advice of a physician, either directly or indirectly. The
intent of the author is only to offer information of a general nature to help you
in your quest for emotional and spiritual well-being. In the event you use any
of the information in this book for yourself, which is your constitutional right,
the author and the publisher assume no responsibility for your actions.

Any people depicted in stock imagery provided by Thinkstock are models,
and such images are being used for illustrative purposes only.
Certain stock imagery © Thinkstock.

Printed in the United States of America

ISBN: 978-1-4525-6871-3 (sc)
ISBN: 978-1-4525-6872-0 (e)

Balboa Press rev. date: 2/13/2013

A Prayer to you before you start your journey.

Your guardians and guides are with me. Sharing to you that they are always with you.

They were chosen to join with you on this journey of your path that you are walking. They also chose to be your protectors. Some are protectors and some are guides, but all of them do it in the name of Love. They are here to assist you, and guide you, to show that Love is always here. You will go through challenges, and are going through challenges, that have already been decided, that you will see through to the light. This is simply a lesson to share with those loved ones whom are also going through this experience. Each one of you is seeing a facet of Love through this trying time. It may not seem that way, but this is the process of a diamond being polished. That diamond is your heart and soul, and it is always capable of miraculous things that our mind never dreamed possible. Your mind is working with you, to show that you must choose your heart to get through these trying times. Every scary thought and every negative vision

I Am 愛

that you receive is just another opportunity to walk away from the path of fear, close that door, and open the door unto the path of peace, tranquility and Love. Your heart has never let you down, and has never failed you.

All of the times that you had hard learned lessons were to verify that you must love You first. Love your heart and soul first, so that you can receive the energy to love and help others.

This prayer is for you and only you. It is your guides that share, that this is the time to put yourself first. Everyone has a heart and soul, but they sometimes forget, so they look towards other people's heart and soul for warmth, and to fill the empty void that they feel. This void is not real, for in it lies love. Every creature on this planet was given a loving heart & soul just for them, but when we stop believing in our own heart, so too does the feeling of love and joy leave our heart. You must re-connect with your heart, for Love gave this gift just for you.

It is this gift of Love from within that will make it possible to face your challenge with Love, Compassion, Patience, Wisdom, & Kindness. You will make it through, and everyone you love and adore will all be ok. Nothing will falter amidst the love, wisdom, and light of Love.

Feel the Love radiate from within, and let it pour out through the rest of your body.

This is the healing and protecting energy of Love.

Your guides will continue to show you how to get there and how to stay there.

All is well.

All is calm.

All is Love.

You are Love, you are Loved, you are protected.

Be well in peace, and walk on your path with confidence knowing that you are not alone.

Feel the warmth in your heart of those that are guiding you and protecting you.

Everyone on this Earth is given a diamond of heart, soul & Love.

Everyone on this Earth are given guides and protectors.

May you walk in Love, Wisdom and Light.

Be blessed for all is given to You.

This is a message written by me, but it is from your guardians and guides.

I Am 愛

I
AM

Pronounced: "I; ái," as in "I," which means "Love."

Through this book, you will learn a poetic way of how we are made in the image and likeness of Love.

Take a journey reconnecting to your heart, to 愛, to Love, to "I."

This book is dedicated to Love.
For the truth will set you free.

How To Use
This Book:

*There are 31 Affirmations, with
a blank page next to it. Each day
you will read one Affirmation, and
take a moment to write down or
draw your feelings and thoughts.*

*You can read more than one affirmation
or you can read them all at once.*

*The important thing is to give
yourself that time after reading the
affirmation, to listen to what your
heart has to say, and to write down
or draw the words or feelings you hear
or feel coming from your heart.*

*Your Heart will only speak words
of Love & Truth. You will only
feel feelings of Love & Truth*

*Any words you hear that are "negative,"
in nature, are not coming from your
heart. They are coming from your
mind. These "negative" words give you
the opportunity to listen to the positive
words coming from your heart.*

*It may take time to hear the whispers
in your heart, but keep following them,
and your life will forever change.*

*May Your Path be Forever
Blessed in the name of Love.*

Feel
Love

*Your heart speaks to you the same
way that your mind does.*

*Your heart speaks all
positive loving words.*

Listen always to your heart.

It is never wrong.

I
AM
愛
Use this page to write or draw your feelings & thoughts.
There are no rules how to do it, that's why there are no lines.

Believe
In
ME

When you believe in you,
you believe in Love.

Love always believes in You!

I
AM
愛
Use this page to write or draw your feelings & thoughts.
There are no rules how to do it, that's why there are no lines.

Believe
In
Myself

You are not just what you see in the mirror.

Believe in the love that you feel inside, for that is your "True You!"

I
AM
愛

Use this page to write or draw your feelings & thoughts.
There are no rules how to do it, that's why there are no lines.

I
Know

Only you know You.

No one else can tell you who You are.

I
AM
愛

Use this page to write or draw your feelings & thoughts.
There are no rules how to do it, that's why there are no lines.

Can

Do

It

If Anyone Can, 愛 Can.

Love can do anything.

With love, I can do anything.

I
AM
愛

Use this page to write or draw your feelings & thoughts.
There are no rules how to do it, that's why there are no lines.

Will
Fail

There is nothing bad about failing.

Ever.

*Failure is the opportunity
to learn a lesson.*

*Failure is the cocoon, waiting to
become the butterfly of success.*

I
AM
愛
Use this page to write or draw your feelings & thoughts.
There are no rules how to do it, that's why there are no lines.

I Am 愛

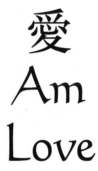

Am
Love

Love Is Perfect.

You Are Love.

You Are Perfect.

I
AM
愛
Use this page to write or draw your feelings & thoughts.
There are no rules how to do it, that's why there are no lines.

Am
Truth

Love Is Truth.

No: "one," "thing," or "body,"

*is ever separated, divided,
or denied Love.*

That's the Truth!

I
AM
愛

Use this page to write or draw your feelings & thoughts.
There are no rules how to do it, that's why there are no lines.

Can
Heal

Love heals everything and anything.

*Love heals from within your heart,
and through your soul & body.*

I
AM
愛

Use this page to write or draw your feelings & thoughts.
There are no rules how to do it, that's why there are no lines.

Can
Forgive

Love yourself.

*Let go of those that have
brought you hurt.*

That is forgiving them.

I
AM
愛

Use this page to write or draw your feelings & thoughts.
There are no rules how to do it, that's why there are no lines.

Am
Compassion

Empathy for others has compassion.

Empathy can see suffering is necessary, & temporary.

Compassion is heartfelt with empathy.

I
AM
愛
Use this page to write or draw your feelings & thoughts.
There are no rules how to do it, that's why there are no lines.

I Am 愛

Am
Trust

*Living a life of morals is
how we learn to trust.*

Morals do not need rules or laws.

Trust in your heart.

Not in your head.

I
AM
愛

Use this page to write or draw your feelings & thoughts.
There are no rules how to do it, that's why there are no lines.

I Am 愛

愛
Am
Kindness

Listen to the whispers of your heart, for they are the guides towards your path.

They will let you know when to be kind.

Kindness is not weakness.

Kindness has the strength to say no.

I
AM
愛
Use this page to write or draw your feelings & thoughts.
There are no rules how to do it, that's why there are no lines.

Am
Patience

Be still in peace and wait for the answers to your hopes and prayers.

They are answered always in the way that they are supposed to.

Never in the way that you expect them.

I
AM
愛
Use this page to write or draw your feelings & thoughts.
There are no rules how to do it, that's why there are no lines.

Am
Faithful

A faithful heart has peace from within.

Be faithful to your heart, and to yourself.

*From there you learn to
be faithful to others.*

I
AM
愛
Use this page to write or draw your feelings & thoughts.
There are no rules how to do it, that's why there are no lines.

I Am 愛

Am

Hope

A faithful heart always has hope, and patience, knowing that all is taken care of.

I
AM
愛

Use this page to write or draw your feelings & thoughts.
There are no rules how to do it, that's why there are no lines.

I Am 愛

Am
Understanding

*Use your heart to understand,
not your mind.*

Love is deeper than logic.

*If a prayer did not get answered,
there is something more important
to learn & understand.*

I
AM
愛

Use this page to write or draw your feelings & thoughts.
There are no rules how to do it, that's why there are no lines.

Am

Knowing

*"True Education" questions everything
and learns what is "Truth."*

This is how to learn "True Knowledge."

I
AM
愛

Use this page to write or draw your feelings & thoughts.
There are no rules how to do it, that's why there are no lines.

Am

Art

Everything created comes from Love.

Everything created is a
perfect work of art.

You are a perfect work of art, and
everything which that you create.

I
AM
愛

Use this page to write or draw your feelings & thoughts.
There are no rules how to do it, that's why there are no lines.

I Am 愛

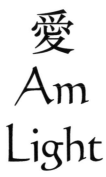

Am
Light

The path of Love is always well lit.

You are the path of light.

You will always shine when on your path.

I
AM
愛

Use this page to write or draw your feelings & thoughts.
There are no rules how to do it, that's why there are no lines.

I Am 愛

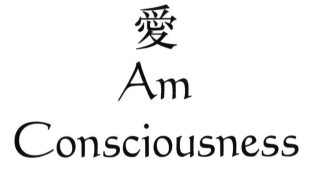

Am
Consciousness

Be aware of everything that you do.

*Admit that you are responsible
for every decision you make.*

This is conciseness.

I
AM
愛

Use this page to write or draw your feelings & thoughts.
There are no rules how to do it, that's why there are no lines.

I Am 愛

The
Way
is

The Path to Love is me.

I am the Path to Love.

Love is the Path to You.

I
AM
愛

Use this page to write or draw your feelings & thoughts.
There are no rules how to do it, that's why there are no lines.

You
Are

You are Love.

You are I.

We are Love.

I
AM
愛

Use this page to write or draw your feelings & thoughts.
There are no rules how to do it, that's why there are no lines.

Am
You

Love is You.

I am you.

We are love.

I
AM
愛

Use this page to write or draw your feelings & thoughts.
There are no rules how to do it, that's why there are no lines.

Love
You

*Love is everything, and you
are a part of everything.*

I
AM
愛

Use this page to write or draw your feelings & thoughts.
There are no rules how to do it, that's why there are no lines.

Am
Forever

Forever Loving is Forever Living.

Love is Forever.

I Am Love.

I Am Forever.

I
AM
愛

Use this page to write or draw your feelings & thoughts.
There are no rules how to do it, that's why there are no lines.

Am
Wisdom

Love Is Wisdom.

I Am Love.

I Am Wisdom.

I
AM
愛

Use this page to write or draw your feelings & thoughts.
There are no rules how to do it, that's why there are no lines.

1

Apply

When you apply Love to True Knowledge, you get Wisdom.

I
AM
愛
Use this page to write or draw your feelings & thoughts.
There are no rules how to do it, that's why there are no lines.

The
Way
Forever
in
Wisdom
is
愛

Forever remain on the Path
of Love, and you Forever
remain on the Path of You.

I
AM
愛

Use this page to write or draw your feelings & thoughts.
There are no rules how to do it, that's why there are no lines.

I Am 愛

God

is

All Ways of Love are Always of God.

God is All Ways of Love.

God is Always of Love.

I
AM
愛

Use this page to write or draw your feelings & thoughts.
There are no rules how to do it, that's why there are no lines.

I
Am

I Am Truth, Knowledge, Wisdom, Patience, Compassion, Empathy, Understanding, Faith, Belief, Forgiveness, Hope, & Healing.

I Am the Way to Love.

God is love.

I am Love.

I
AM
愛

Use this page to write or draw your feelings & thoughts.
There are no rules how to do it, that's why there are no lines.

I Am 愛